I Like Science! Bilingual

Visitando volcanes con una científica

Visiting Volcanoes with a Scientist

Catherine McGlone

Enslow Elementary
an imprint of
Enslow Publishers, Inc.
40 Industrial Road
Box 398
Berkeley Heights, NJ 07922
USA

http://www.enslow.com

Contents

Contenido

Words to Know / Palabras a conocer

earthquake (URTH kwayk)—A shaking of the ground. Earthquakes happen when rock moves below the earth's surface.

erupt (ee RUPT)—To explode, as when lava shoots out of the hole of a volcano.

lava (LAH vuh)—Melted rock coming from a volcano or crack in the earth.

magma (MAG muh)—Melted rock inside the earth.

mineral (MIHN ur uhl)—A solid natural substance, like a diamond, that comes out of the ground.

volcano (vahl KAY noh)—An opening in the earth's surface where lava, pieces of rock, and hot gas come out. Most volcanoes look like mountains.

terremoto—Temblor del suelo. Los terremotos ocurren cuando se mueven las rocas debajo de la superficie de la tierra.

hacer erupción—Explotar, como cuando un volcán lanza lava.

lava—Roca fundida que sale de un volcán o de una grieta en la tierra.

magma—Roca fundida dentro de la tierra.

mineral—Una sustancia sólida natural, como un diamante, que sale del suelo.

volcán—Una apertura en la superficie de la tierra por donde salen lava, pedazos de roca y gas caliente. La mayoría de los volcanes tienen forma de montaña.

Imagine how surprised people were the first time they saw a volcano erupt. They must have had many questions.

Imagina la sorpresa de las personas que vieron un volcán hacer erupción por primera vez. Deben haberse hecho muchas preguntas.

Meet Cynthia Gardner.

She is a volcano scientist. She finds out how volcanoes work. She learns about volcanoes by asking questions.

Ella es Cynthia Gardner.

Es científica de volcanes. Ella investiga cómo funcionan los volcanes. Aprende sobre los volcanes haciendo preguntas.

4

She tells people who live near volcanoes what might happen when a volcano erupts.

Les dice a las personas que viven cerca de los volcanes lo que puede ocurrir cuando un volcán hace erupción.

What is a volcano?

Hot gas, melted rock, and bits of rock blow out of a hole in the earth.

¿Qué es un volcán?

Gas caliente, roca fundida y pedazos de roca salen por un agujero de la tierra.

The rock cools and piles up around the hole. This forms a volcano.

La roca se enfría y va formando montones alrededor del agujero. Así se forma un volcán.

Some volcanoes are very small. Others erupt over and over again and grow to be large mountains.

Algunos volcanes son muy pequeños. Otros hacen erupción una y otra vez y crecen hasta convertirse en montañas grandes.

Why are there volcanoes?

The inside of the earth is very hot. To cool off, the earth lets go of the heat. Heat melts the earth's rock. The melted rock is called magma.

magma

¿Por qué hay volcanes?

El interior de la tierra es muy caliente. Para enfriarse, la tierra deja escapar el calor. El calor funde la roca de la tierra. A la roca fundida se le llama magma.

When magma comes out of the volcano, it is called lava.

Cuando el magma sale del volcán, se le llama lava.

9

When will a volcano erupt?

Scientists look for clues.
Often there are earthquakes
under the volcano.

¿Cuándo hará erupción un volcán?

Los científicos buscan pistas. Con
frecuencia hay terremotos debajo
del volcán.

Many times the volcano sends gas out of its hole. Sometimes the volcano gets fatter or thinner.

Muchas veces el volcán lanza gas por su agujero. A veces el volcán se hace más grueso o más delgado.

Mt. St. Helens, 1980, a few weeks before it erupted / Monte Santa Helena, 1980, semanas antes de hacer erupción

11

How do scientists find these clues?

They use special tools that measure the gas. The tools tell how much gas is coming out of the volcano.

¿Cómo encuentran los científicos estas pistas?

Usan herramientas especiales que miden el gas. Las herramientas les dicen cuánto gas está saliendo del volcán.

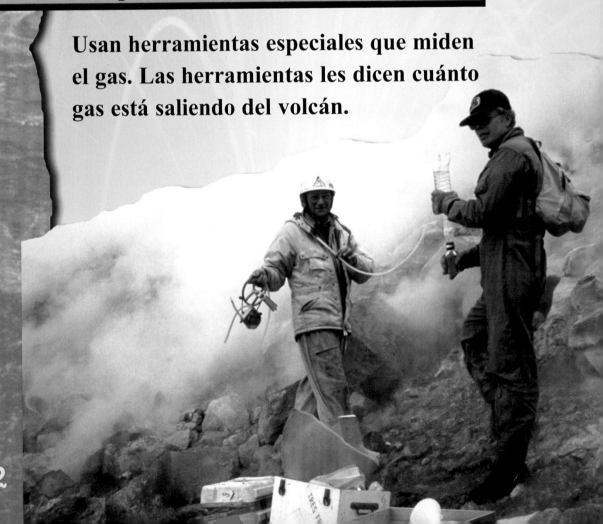

A lot of gas is a clue that the volcano may be ready to erupt.

Una gran cantidad de gas es una pista de que el volcán puede estar listo para hacer erupción.

What else does scientist Cynthia do?

Scientist Cynthia looks at rocks she finds on volcanoes. She breaks the rocks open and looks at them with a hand lens.

¿Qué más hace la científica Cynthia?

La científica Cynthia mira las rocas que encuentra en los volcanes. Abre las rocas y las mira con una lupa.

minerals/minerales

There are minerals inside the rock. The rock was made deep inside the earth. The minerals show just how deep the rocks were.

Dentro de la roca hay minerales. La roca se hizo en lo profundo de la tierra. Los minerales muestran a qué profundidad estaban las rocas.

What tools does scientist Cynthia use?

Scientist Cynthia writes about the clues she finds in her notebook. She carries the notebook in her backpack, along with her shovel, hammer, and drinking water.

¿Qué herramientas usa la científica Cynthia?

La científica Cynthia escribe las pistas que encuentra en su cuaderno. Lleva su cuaderno en la mochila, junto con una pala, un martillo y agua para beber.

16

She uses the clues she finds to make maps of the volcano area.

Usa las pistas que encuentra para hacer mapas del área del volcán.

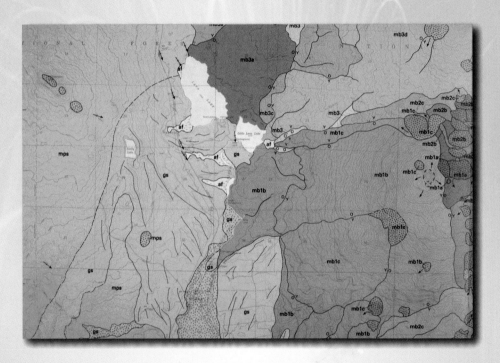

Cynthia made this map. It shows different areas of lava that came out of volcanoes in Oregon. Each color stands for a different age of lava. / Cynthia hizo este mapa. Muestra diferentes áreas de lava que salieron de los volcanes de Oregon. Cada color representa una edad diferente de la lava.

Where are volcanoes found?

Volcanoes are found around the world. Most volcanoes are in the Ring of Fire. Scientist Cynthia has visited volcanoes in many places.

¿Dónde hay volcanes?

Hay volcanes en todo el mundo. La mayoría de los volcanes están en el Círculo de Fuego. La científica Cynthia ha visitado volcanes en muchos lugares.

Sometimes she looks at volcanoes from a helicopter. She loves being outdoors to do her job!

A veces mira los volcanes desde un helicóptero. ¡Le gusta estar al aire libre para hacer su trabajo!

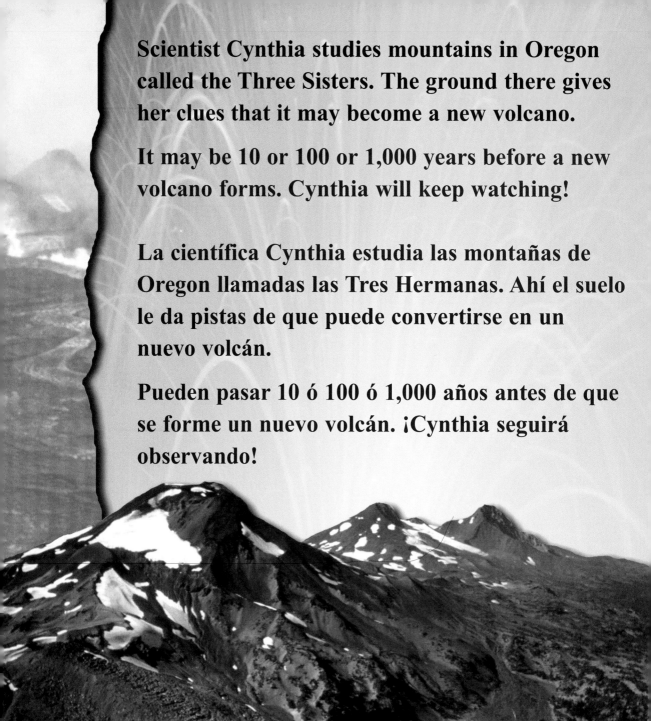

Scientist Cynthia studies mountains in Oregon called the Three Sisters. The ground there gives her clues that it may become a new volcano.

It may be 10 or 100 or 1,000 years before a new volcano forms. Cynthia will keep watching!

La científica Cynthia estudia las montañas de Oregon llamadas las Tres Hermanas. Ahí el suelo le da pistas de que puede convertirse en un nuevo volcán.

Pueden pasar 10 ó 100 ó 1,000 años antes de que se forme un nuevo volcán. ¡Cynthia seguirá observando!

Can you make your own volcano?

You will need:

- ✔ empty yogurt cup
- ✔ baking sheet
- ✔ play dough or clay
- ✔ measuring cup
- ✔ water
- ✔ tablespoon
- ✔ baking soda
- ✔ vinegar

1. Place an empty yogurt cup on a baking sheet.

2. Mold play dough or clay into a volcano shape around the yogurt cup. Leave the opening at the top uncovered.

3. Pour $\frac{1}{4}$ cup of water into the container. Stir in 1 tablespoon of baking soda.

4. Pour $\frac{1}{4}$ cup of vinegar into the container.

5. Watch what happens!

What happens if you repeat the experiment and add less vinegar? What happens if you add more vinegar?

¿Puedes hacer tu propio volcán?

Necesitarás:

- ✔ un vaso de yogurt vacío
- ✔ bandeja para hornear
- ✔ plastilina
- ✔ taza medidora
- ✔ agua
- ✔ cuchara
- ✔ bicarbonato
- ✔ vinagre

1. Coloca un vaso de yogurt vacío en una bandeja para hornear.

2. Haz un volcán de plastilina alrededor del vaso de yogurt. Deja abierta la parte de arriba.

3. Vacía $\frac{1}{4}$ de taza de agua en el recipiente. Mezcla 1 cucharada de bicarbonato.

4. Vacía $\frac{1}{4}$ de taza de vinagre en el recipiente.

5. ¡Observa lo que ocurre!

¿Qué ocurre si repites el experimento y añades menos vinagre? ¿Qué ocurre si añades más vinagre?

Learn More / Más para aprender

Books / Libros

In English / En inglés

Berger, Melvin, and Gilda Berger. *Why Do Volcanoes Blow Their Tops?* New York: Scholastic, Inc., 2000.

Durbin, Christopher. *Volcanoes*. San Diego, Calif.: Blackbirch Press, 2004.

O'Meara, Donna. *Into the Volcano: A Volcano Researcher at Work*. Toronto, Canada: Kids Can Press, 2005.

In Spanish / En español

Asimov, Isaac. *La tierra*. Milwaukee, Wisc.: Gareth Stevens Pub., 2004.

Internet Addresses / Direcciones de Internet

In English / En inglés

University of North Dakota. *Volcano World*.
<http://volcano.und.nodak.edu>

United States Geological Survey.
<http://volcanoes.usgs.gov>

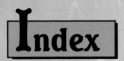

Index

Índice

❧ To my favorite young readers—Jimmy, Mick, Brendan, Joseph, and Mary Cate ❧

Note to Teachers and Parents: The *I Like Science!* series supports the National Science Education Standards for K–4 science, including content standards "Science as a human endeavor" and "Science as inquiry." The Words to Know section introduces subject-specific vocabulary, including pronunciation and definitions. Early readers may require help with these new words.

Enslow Elementary, an imprint of Enslow Publishers, Inc.
Enslow Elementary® is a registered trademark of Enslow Publishers, Inc.

Bilingual edition copyright 2008 by Enslow Publishers, Inc. Originally published in English under the title *Visiting Volcanoes with a Scientist* © 2004 by Enslow Publishers, Inc. Bilingual edition translated by Nora Díaz, edited by María Cristina Mella, of Strictly Spanish, LLC.

Library of Congress Cataloging-in-Publication Data

McGlone, Catherine.
  [Visiting volcanoes with a scientist. Spanish & English]
  Visitando volcanes con una científica = Visiting volcanoes with a scientist / Catherine McGlone. — Bilingual ed.
    p. cm. — (I like science! Bilingual)
  Summary: "Discusses the science of volcanoes"—Provided by publisher.
  Includes bibliographical references and index.
  ISBN-13: 978-0-7660-2979-8
  ISBN-10: 0-7660-2979-4
  1. Volcanoes—Juvenile literature. I. Title.
QE521.3.M39218 2008
551.21—dc22

2007011640

Printed in the United States of America

10 9 8 7 6 5 4 3 2 1

To Our Readers: We have done our best to make sure all Internet Addresses in this book were active and appropriate when we went to press. However, the author and the publisher have no control over and assume no liability for the material available on those Internet sites or on other Web sites they may link to. Any comments or suggestions can be sent by e-mail to comments@enslow.com or to the address on the back cover.

Photo Credits: © 2002–2003 ArtToday.com, Inc., p. 6; © 1999 Artville, LLC, p. 18; Enslow Publishers, Inc. pp. 21, 22; Gary Hincks/Science Photo Library, p. 8; Dr. Juerg Alean/Science Photo Library, p. 9; United States Department of the Interior, U. S. Geological Survey, David A. Johnston Cascades Volcano Observatory, Vancouver, Washington, pp.1, 2, 4, 15, 17, 19, 22, Thomas J. Casadevall, p. 12; B. Chouet, pp. 3, 13, 20–21; Austin Post, p. 7; W. E. Scott, pp. 5, 14, 16; Donald A. Swanson, pp. 10–11.

Cover Photo: United States Department of the Interior, U. S. Geological Survey, David A. Johnston Cascades Volcano Observatory, Vancouver, Washington.

A special thanks to David Wieprecht for his help in obtaining the illustrations.

Series Literacy Consultant:
Allan A. De Fina, Ph.D.
Past President of the New Jersey Reading Association
Professor, Department of Literacy Education
New Jersey City University

Science Consultant:
Cynthia Gardner, Geologist
U.S. Geological Survey
Cascades Volcano Observatory